Suzuki Violin School
™
VIOLIN PART
VOLUME 5

™

Copyright © 1978 by Zen-On Music Company, Ltd.
Tokyo, Japan
Sole publisher for the entire world except Japan:
Summy-Birchard Inc.
exclusively distributed by
Warner Bros. Publications Inc.
265 Secaucus Road
Secaucus, New Jersey 07096-2037
All rights reserved   Printed in U.S.A.

ISBN 0-87487-152-2
9   11   13   15   14   12   10

The Suzuki name, logo and wheel device
are trademarks of Summy-Birchard Inc.

CONTENTS

(No. 1 is unaccompanied)

Tonalization
トナリゼイション

Tonalisation   **Tonführung**   Sonidización

毎レッスン指導

美しい音とビブラートの練習

Tonalization exercises should be practiced at each lesson.
Exercise for beautiful tone and vibrato.

Les exercices de tonalisation devraient être exécutés à chaque leçon.
Exercice pour obtenir un beau ton et un beau vibrato.

Tonführung-Übungen sollten in jeder Unterrichtsstunde geübt werden.
Übung für schönen Ton und Vibrato.

Los ejercicios de sonidización deben ser practicados en cada lección.
Ejercicio para tono y vibrato hermoso.

𝑓 (フォルテ) と 𝑝 (ピアノ) の練習

Exercise for forte and piano   *Übungen für forte und piano*

Exercice pour forte et piano   Ejercicios para forte y piano

1. 𝑓 ＝ (Ｂ) の位置 (駒の近く) を弓を最後までまっすぐにひく。

2. 𝑝 ＝ (Ａ) の位置をまっすぐにひく。

音色と音量の変化に注意すること。

1. **For forte: Place the bow near the bridge (B) and use a whole, straight bow.**
2. **For piano: Place the bow away from the bridge (A) and use a whole, straight bow.**

1. *Pour forte: Placer l'archet près du chevalet (B) et utiliser tout l'archet dans un coup droit.*
2. *Pour piano: Placer l'archet loin du chevalet (A) et utiliser tout l'archet dans un coup droit.*

1. *Für forte: Den Bogen nahe dem Steg (B) setzen und einen ganzen, geraden Bogenstrich gebrauchen.*
2. *Für piano: Den Bogen weiter weg vom Steg (A) setzen und einen ganzen, geraden Bogenstrich gebrauchen.*

1. Para forte: Coloque el arco cerca del puente (B) y arquee en una línea recta, en su totalidad.
2. Para piano: Coloque el arco lejos del puente (A) y emplee el arco derecho, en su totalidad.

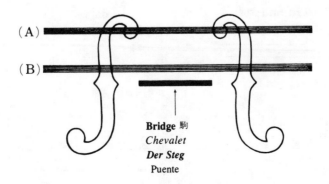

Bridge 駒
Chevalet
Der Steg
Puente

Position Etude, 4th position

ポジション・エチュード　第4ポジション

Etude de Position, 4ème position　　　**Lagen-Etüde, vierte Lage**　　　Estudio de Posición, 4ta posición

II

E String   *Corde du mi*   **E-Saite**   Cuerda mi

A String   *Corde du la*   **A-Saite**   Cuerda la

D String   *Corde du ré*   **D-Saite**   Cuerda re

G String   *Corde du sol*   **G-Saite**   Cuerda sol

2.10.98

1

Gavotte

ガボット

Gavotte I

Allegro moderato

J. S. Bach
バッハ

Gavotte II

D.C. Gavotte I

2.10.98

Concerto in A Minor
2nd Movement

ラルゴ

「協奏曲イ短調」から

A.Vivaldi
ビバルディ

Etude for Changing Strings

移弦の練習曲

Etude pour le changement des cordes   **Etüde für Saitenwechsel**   Estudio para el cruzar de cuerdas

Shinichi Suzuki

速度は速すぎないように注意し，確実な音とテンポでひく。

Try to maintain a constant tone and tempo, taking care not to get too fast.

Essayer de maintenir le ton et le tempo de manière constante, en faisant attention à ne pas aller trop vite.

Versuche, einen gleichmässigen Ton und Tempo durchzuhalten, gib Acht, nicht zu schnell zu werden.

Trate de mantener un tono constante y un tiempo constante, esforzándose por no hacerlo demasiado ligero.

Position Etude, 5th Position
ポジション・エチュード　第５ポジション
Etude de Position, 5ème position　　　*Lagen-Etüde, fühfte Lage*　　　Estudio de Posición, 5ta posición

10

16

sul E

Solo

p grazioso

mf

p dolce

cresc.

poco allargando

Tutti *a tempo*

p

f

f

sul E

p

dolce

tr

Solo

p leggiero

mf

dolce

* 記法
written
écrit
geschrieben
escrito

奏法
played
joué
gespielt
tocado

4

Country Dance

カントリー ダンス

C. M. von Weber
ウェーバー

Danse Champêtre   ***Ländlicher Tanz***   Danza Campestre

5

German Dance

ドイツ舞曲

K. D. von Dittersdorf
ディッタースドルフ

Danse Allemande   ***Deutscher Tanz***   Danza Alemana

6

Gigue from Sonata in D Minor

ジーガ 「ソナタ二短調」から

Allegro Vivace

F.M.Veracini
ベラチーニ

Gigue de la Sonate en ré mineur   ***Gigue aus Sonate in D-Moll***

Giga de la Sonata en re menor

7

Concerto for Two Violins
1st Movement

ビバーチェ
「二つのバイオリンのための協奏曲」から
第1バイオリン

Violin I

J. S. Bach
バッハ

Concerto pour Deux Violons, Ier mouvement

Konzert für zwei Geigen, Erster Satz　　Concierto para Dos Violines, 1er movimiento